Terrance Talks Travel:
The Quirky Tourist Guide to Reykjavik (Iceland)

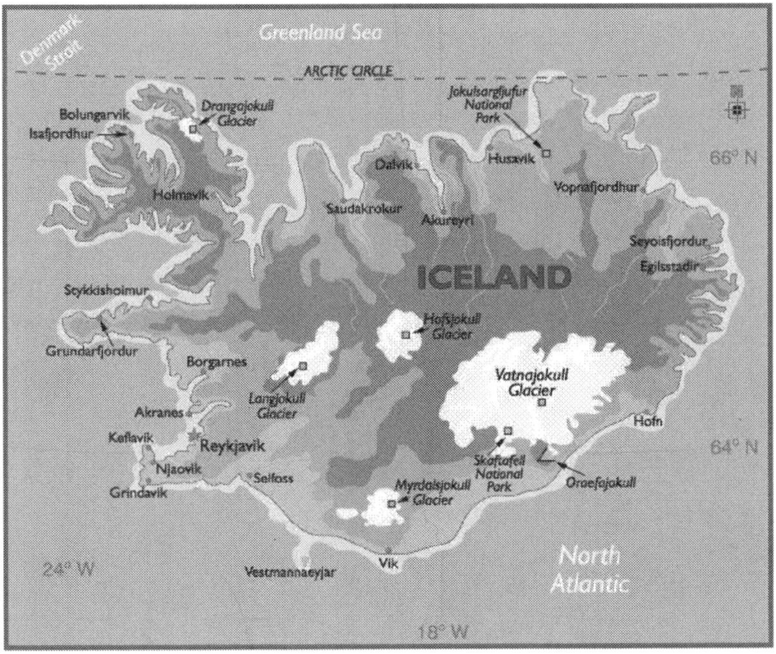

Terrance Zepke

TERRANCE TALKS TRAVEL: The Quirky Tourist Guide to Reykjavik | Terrance Zepke

Copyright © 2018 by Terrance Zepke

All rights reserved. No part of this book shall be reproduced or transmitted in any form or by any means, electronic, mechanical, magnetic, and photographic including photocopying, recording or by any information storage and retrieval system, without prior written permission of the publisher. No patent liability is assumed with respect to the use of the information contained herein. Although every precaution has been taken in the preparation of this book, the publisher and author assume no responsibility for errors or omissions. Neither is any liability assumed for damages resulting from the use of the information contained herein.

All queries should be directed to: www.safaripublishing.net.

For more about the author, www.terrancezepke.com and www.terrancetalkstravel.com.

ISBN-13: 978-1942738411
ISBN-10: 1942738412

TERRANCE TALKS TRAVEL: The Quirky Tourist Guide to Reykjavik | Terrance Zepke

Library of Congress Cataloging-in-Publication Data

America/Zepke, Terrance p.cm.

Terrance Talks Travel: The Quirky Tourist Guide to Reykjavik

1. Travel-Iceland. 2. Adventure Travel. 3. Reykjavik. 4. Northern Lights. 5. Blue Lagoon. 6. Reykjavik Guidebook. 7. Europe-Travel. 8. Iceland Waterfalls, Glaciers, and National Parks. 9. Iceland Guidebook. 10. Iceland Attractions. I. Title.

First edition

Safari Publishing

TERRANCE TALKS TRAVEL: The Quirky Tourist Guide to
Reykjavik | Terrance Zepke

CONTENTS

Introduction, 5
Getting There & Getting Around, 9
Fast Facts, 13
Terrance's Top Ten Picks, 17
Touristy Things to See & Do, 35
Best of Reykjavik, 61
About Accommodations, 83
About Iceland, 90
Annual Events & Average Temps, 98
What to Pack, 120
Titles by Terrance, 124
Index, 147

INTRODUCTION

Are you a quirky tourist? You are if you like to see and do different kinds of things than the average tourist. The average tourist goes sightseeing. The quirky tourist *travels*. He immerses himself in the local culture. He likes offbeat places, weird attractions, and adventurous activities.

In this reference, I have included all the usual touristy stuff because most of us want to do those things. Who wants to go to Paris and not visit the Eiffel Tower or go to New York City and not see Times Square?

But some of us are searching for more. You know who you are. You are willing to go miles out of your way to see oddities, such as

Iceland's Elf School and the Phallological Museum. You scour the Internet before every trip searching for anything out of the ordinary. You seek out local delicacies, choosing to eat foods you can't even pronounce, but be forewarned that you need to be Anthony Zimmern to eat some of Iceland's bizarre cuisine! You like places with irresistible and unusual gimmicks. I'll reveal a fun Vikings theme restaurant that may be right up your alley, not to mention an adorable laundromat that is also a bar, café, and bookstore—and serves the best Sunday brunch.

Quirky travelers embrace new experiences. You have your limits but are game for anything that is not too physically challenging or too extreme. Quirky locals are drawn to you, which is good because there's nothing you love more than meeting colorful characters. You dare to trod off the beaten path and see what happens.

Good for you! That's what travel is all about. And that's what this book is all about. I reveal the best of Iceland, which is an awful lot considering this is a small Nordic island nation the size of Kentucky. But it is packed with quirkiness! There are volcano tours, scuba diving in Silfra, ice cave lava tours, the legendary Blue Lagoon (a must do!), Hallgrimskirkja (a must see!), and a one-of-a-kind man-made geothermal beach area. I also reveal the best dance club, coziest bar, best foodie tour, unique lodging, and much more. Learn what a "Rüntur" is and discover a highly rated spa treatment that uses fish in such a weird way that it is banned in the U.S.

Two-thirds of Iceland's population resides in the capital city of Reykjavik, which is also one of the smallest capitals in the world. Even so, it has six districts and a population of more than 230,000. While there is more to Iceland than Reykjavik, ninety-five percent of its tourist attractions are in the greater Reykjavik area.

So read on to learn how to make the most out of your time in the Republic of Iceland. Pay special attention to my TOP TEN PICKS, Annual Events, and FYI boxes.

GETTING THERE

You can only get to Iceland by boat or plane. The flight averages 5-6 hours from North America and 3-4 hours from Europe.

By Air

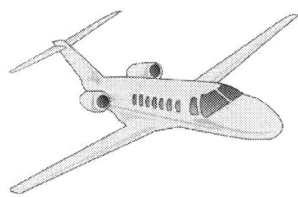

While there are thirteen commercial airports in Iceland, most tourists will arrive at Reykjavik International Airport, http://www.isavia.is/english/airports/reykjavik-international-airport/, or Keflavik International Airport, http://www.kefairport.is/english/. Icelandair is the national airline of Iceland and it operates flights to thirty-one cities in thirteen countries. www.icelandair.com.

Other options include:

www.britishairways.com

www.delta.com

www.wowair.com

www.easyJet.com

www.whizair.com

www.airberlin.com

www.thomson.co.uk

www.flysas.com

www.finnair.com

www.klm.com

www.norweigan.com

www.austrian.com

www.flyniki.com

www.airgreenland.com

www.iberia.com

By Ferry

There is limited ferry service to the island. For a schedule of times and locations, www.smyrilline.com.

Getting Around Iceland

Bus: Reykjavík has an extensive network of local buses connecting all the suburbs, and running to Akranes, Borgarnes, Hveragerði, Selfoss, and Hvalfjarðarsveit. See www.straeto.is for information on routes, fares, and timetables.

Taxi: Most taxis in Iceland operate in the Reykjavík area. Beware that taxis are metered, and the fare can add up quickly. But the good news is that tipping is not expected.

Car Services & Rentals: There are no Uber and Lyft services here at this time. Cars (and bikes) can be rented. There are can rental agencies at the airport and in Reykjavik.
https://guidetoiceland.is/iceland-car-rentals.

Trains: There is no train system.

Fast Facts

Country Size: 40,000 square miles (roughly the same size as Kentucky and Cuba)

Capital: Reykjavík

Median age: 35

Population: 329,100

Currency: Icelandic Króna (ISK)

Official Language: Icelandic (but English is commonly spoken)

Time Zone: Iceland is on Greenwich Mean Time (GMT) and does not go on daylight saving time.

Nickname: Land of Fire & Ice

Leading Export: Seafood

Flag of Iceland

Documentation: All tourists except those from Scandinavian countries are required to have a passport to enter the country. Visas are not required for most tourists, but citizens of some countries will have to apply for a visa to visit Iceland. Check this list to find out if you need a visa to enter the country. http://utl.is/index.php/en/who-needs-a-visa.

FYI: Iceland is one of the few European countries without rabies. Therefore, traveling to Iceland with your beloved dog or cat requires an application process with several forms, an import application fee, and four weeks of quarantine.

Best Time to Visit: It depends on what you want to do. If you want to see the Northern Lights, enjoy certain activities like snowmobiling, or participate in Christmas celebrations, you will need to go in the winter. If you want to go hiking, horseback riding, or explore national parks, it is best to go during the summer. Most campsites are closed during the winter. For many, the ideal time will be May – September because the days are long during those months. It is best to avoid the fall as that is when they have the most precipitation. Some think the best month is July. On the other hand, I enjoy visiting Iceland in the winter, but I stay in the Reykjavik area, opting not to drive around the country during those months due to the snowy winters. However, it is perfect for seeing the Northern Lights, pampering yourself spa treatments, and partaking in special seasonal celebrations, including Christmas shopping at the Christmas Market. From late November – early January, there are candles, lights, and decorations everywhere, so Iceland is a picture perfect winter wonderland.

TERRANCE'S TOP TEN PICKS

1. **Complete the Golden Circle.** This is a 190-mile loop that starts and ends in Reykjavik. It takes 6-8 hours to complete. During this exciting excursion, you will visit the highlights or "golden" attractions of Iceland. This includes three main stops:

Thingvellir National Park (a UNESCO World Heritage Site that is also known as Þingvellir National Park), Gullfoss Waterfall, and Haukadalur (includes Geysir and Strokkur geysers). Other stops include the Kerio Volcanic Crater Lake, Skalholt Cathedral, Hverageroi (town), and Nesjavellir and Hellisheioarvikjun geothermal power plants.

2. **Take a self-drive adventure on the Ring Road** (also known as Route 1) is the national road that extends across Iceland. It makes a circle or ring around the island, hence the name. Some visitors choose to self-drive part or all of it (832 miles total) and see some of the country's best attractions on their own, such as Skogafoss

Waterfall, Blue Lagoon, Thingvellir, Dettifoss, Gullfoss, and Jokulsarlon glacier lagoon. Ring Road passes through six tourist highlights: (1) Reykjavik, (2) Borgarnes, (3) Blonduos, (4) Akureyri, (5) Egilsstaoir, (6) Hofn, and (7) Selfoss. You will need at least a week in Iceland if you plan to drive all of the Ring Road. This is because you cannot average more than forty miles per hour and you must allow time for unexpected stops. In addition to stopping at all the usual attractions, you will find a few little-known places you'll want to stop and explore and photo stops you hadn't planned. Here is a suggested itinerary,
http://www.hostel.is/media/PDF/ICELAND_ON_THE_RING_ROAD__essentials_7_days.pdf.

FYI: The Golden Circle is a mini-version of the full Ring Road excursion. If you only have a day to see the highlights, the Golden Circle is the way to go. But if you have a week or more, Ring Road will show you much more of Iceland.

3. **See Rudolph up close**. The eastern part of Iceland is the only place you'll find reindeer in this Nordic nation. There are approximately 3,000 wild reindeer in Iceland. Their primary habitat is in the deserted expanses by Snæfell, but reindeer are seen every year from as far north as Vopnafjördur to as far south as Glacier Lagoon. The best places to view reindeer herds during the summer are the areas around Mount Snæfell, in Vesturöræfi, and Brúaröræfi.

https://www.icelandtravel.is/tour/item691880/reindeer-safari-from-egilsstadir-east-iceland/.

If reindeer aren't your thing, how about a dog-sledding adventure? Greenlandic dogs are tough and hardy sled dogs. Dog-sledding tours are available in the summer and winter or up the ante by dogsledding on an Icelandic glacier, which is an extreme experience! (Sept – April).

https://www.extremeiceland.is/en/activity-tours-iceland/dog-sledding/

4. **Explore Þingvellir National Park** (also known as Thingvellir) where you can find adorable Icelandic Horses. You'll also see sheep and can snorkel too in the summer months. Þingvellir is a site of historical, cultural, and geological significance, and is

one of the most popular tourist destinations in Iceland and a UNESCO World Heritage Site. The park, established in 1930, lies in a rift valley that marks the boundary between the North American tectonic plate and the Eurasian. To its south lies Þingvallavatn, the largest natural lake in Iceland.

http://www.thingvellir.is/english.aspx

5. **Visit Iceland Expo Pavilion.** This is a 360° cinematic experience that shares the best of Iceland. This unique and expensive attraction was created for the World's Fair in 2010. It is now located in Harpa where more than three million visitors have enjoyed seeing this fantastic film. For fifteen thrilling minutes, participants will

venture over erupting volcanos, through waterfalls, view wildlife up close, and go into the heart of Iceland. Shows are every thirty minutes, www.harpa.is.

6. **Take a soak in the Blue Lagoon.** This is a world famous man-made lagoon. It is full of water that is extracted from underground hot springs every two days. It is therapeutic because it is rich in Silica, Sulphur, and other minerals that are beneficial for skin and overall health. In fact, some folks who suffer skin ailments, such as eczema and psoriasis, come to Iceland just to soak in the healing waters of the Blue Lagoon. In addition to soaking in the lagoon, visitors may enjoy spa

treatments, massages, and purchase Blue Lagoon products in their gift shop. There is also a bar and café. The water temperature is always 98-102°F (37-39°C).

7. **See the Aurora Borealis**. In the northern hemisphere, the aurora season runs from early October to late March. The lights may be seen at any time during this period, but late November and February are the best bets. To book a Northern Lights Snowmobiling Adventure, https://www.viator.com/tours/Reykjavik/Northern-Lights-Tour-by-Snowmobile-on-Langjoekull-Glacier-from-Reykjavik/d905-14644P2

FYI: What are Northern Lights? The bright dancing lights of the aurora are collisions between electrically charged particles from the sun that enter the earth's atmosphere. The lights are seen above the magnetic poles of the northern and southern hemispheres. Aurora displays appear in many colors although pale green and pink are the most common. Shades of red, yellow, green, blue, and violet have been reported as streamers, arcs, rippling curtains, or shooting rays that light up the sky with an eerie glow.

8. For those traveling during the spring, summer, or early fall, you can still see the Aurora Borealis—**or rather you can do the next best thing by visiting the Aurora Reykjavik (Northern Lights Center)**. The center features an IMAX-style time-lapse video of the Aurora, which includes myths and legends surrounding the mysterious phenomenon. There's also a Northern Lights simulator and other interactive exhibits. Aurora Reykjavik is at the Reykjavik harbor and is open year round for a fee.

TERRANCE TALKS TRAVEL: The Quirky Tourist Guide to Reykjavik | Terrance Zepke

FYI: In Roman myths, Aurora was the goddess of the dawn. In medieval times, the occurrences of Aurora were seen as harbingers of war or famine. The Maori of New Zealand shared a belief with many northern people of Europe and North America that the lights were reflections from torches or campfires. The Menominee Indians believed that the lights indicated the location of manabai'wok (giants) who were the spirits of great hunters and fishermen. The Alaskan Inuit believed that the lights were the spirits of the animals they hunted. The Aboriginal believed that the lights were the spirits of their people.

9. **Visit The Museum of Icelandic Sorcery & Witchcraft.** At Strandagaldur, there is a museum catering to those fascinated with all things magical. The museum focuses on the elaborate and esoteric spells used in sorcery and contains a collection of Icelandic artifacts and displays, such as runes and staves. There are some bizarre displays and strange ingredients used to concoct certain Icelandic spells. http://www.galdrasyning.is/index.php?lang=en

Icelandic Wonders is tied for #9 on my top picks. This ghosts, elves, and Northern Lights museum is fascinating, informative, and lots of fun! There's even a ghost maze and short film about the Aurora Borealis. It is located in Stokkseyri on the southern coast of Iceland. Plus, there is a souvenir shop, café, and bar where you can enjoy warm waffles and cold beer! http://icelandicwonders.is/

10. **Go to Elf School**. You will learn all about elves and hidden people, as well as gnomes, dwarfs, fairies, trolls, mountain spirits, and other mythical beings. You will have so much fun learning about Icelandic folklore (taught by experts in the field), including a tour of places where elves have been spotted, and you will get fed too. We're talking delicious homemade bread with jam and pancakes with whipped cream! http://www.theelfschool.com/

 **FYI:** More than fifty percent of Icelanders believe in elves. The origin of Elves in Iceland goes back to Germanic paganism and mythology, they were originally a race of minor gods associated with nature and fertility. The elves are usually invisible, but can be seen if they feel like it.

Regional Recipes

Get in the mindset for your trip by sampling some classic Icelandic cuisine. Here are two traditional recipes.

Plokkfiskur is a fish pie (Serves four for main course or eight for starter course if you just want to sample this entree)

1 ¼ lbs. cod, halibut or haddock

1 ¼ lb. potatoes, boiled and peeled

1 white onion

12 oz. milk

2 oz. butter

3 tbsp. flour

salt & pepper (according to taste)

2 tbsp. chives (optional garnish)

Skin, bone & chop the fish into large flakes.
Dice potatoes & finely chop onion.
Heat milk to an almost boil in a small or medium-sized nonstick saucepan.
In a large non-stick saucepan, melt butter & sauté onion over medium-heat until soft—do not allow it to brown.
Sprinkle flour over onion, stirring well & cook for 1-2
minutes.
Gradually add the warmed milk. Simmer for five minutes, stirring often.
Add flaked fish and potatoes and stir until well mixed and thoroughly heated.
Season with salt & pepper and serve with rye or brown bread.

Classic Christmas Cookies

5 ½ cups of flour
1 cup brown sugar
1 cup butter
2 eggs
1 tsp. baking soda
2 tsp. cinnamon
2 tsp. ginger
1 tsp. cloves
1 tsp. baking powder

Similar to ginger snaps, these cookies are delicious. Once the butter reaches room temperature, cut into small pieces (do not melt) and mix in the rest of the ingredients until well mixed. Make small balls and press them down with fork. Bake for 10-15 minutes or until done at 375°F.

FYI: Local dishes: Icelandic food focuses on fish, lamb, and game. A lot of it is traditionally preserved and includes smoked and salted lamb, dried fish, smoked salmon, and cured shark.

A little-known fact is that among the country's most popular foods is the hot dog. The Icelandic version is made from lamb. These are traditionally served with raw and fried onions, ketchup, a slightly sweet brown mustard and remoulade. They are delicious! One of the more bizarre foods in this country is **hákarl**. This is a fermented shark. The unfermented shark is toxic and can kill you. This particular sea creature lacks kidneys, so the fish is left hanging for months to drain the urea from its body before being cured. It is a toss-up as to which is worse—the smell or the taste!

More local delicacies include minke whale (similar in taste and texture to beef), puffin (I'm told it tastes a bit like pastrami), and Skyr. This is classified as a soft cheese. However, it is comparable in taste and texture to Greek Yogurt. It is low in fat and high in protein and calcium.

TOURISTY THINGS TO SEE & DO

Elf School. You will learn all about elves and hidden people, as well as gnomes, dwarfs, fairies, trolls, mountain spirits, and other mythical beings. You will have so much fun learning about Icelandic folklore from experts in the field, including a tour of places where elves have been spotted, and you will get fed too (we're talking delicious homemade bread with jam and pancakes with whipped cream)! http://www.theelfschool.com/

Ellidaardalur Valley is a popular place for anglers, walkers, and cyclists. Arctic char, salmon, and brown trout can be found in the river. A fishing license is needed and fishing season is June 1 – August 31. Fishing can also be done in nearby Reynisvatn and Ellioavatn Lakes.

HALLGRÍMSKIRKJA Church (pictured here) is one of the most beautiful buildings I've ever seen and certainly Reykjavik's best landmark. It can be seen from anywhere in the city. It was designed in 1937, but construction did not begin until 1945. Remarkably, it was not finished until 1986. The crypt was built in 1948, the steeple in 1974, and the nave was consecrated in 1986. Its enormous 50-foot tall and 25-ton pipe organ, built by German organ builder Johannes Klais, is renowned. The church is open every day from 9 a.m. – 5 p.m. This is the most visited attraction in Reykjavik. Admission to the Evangelical-Lutheran church is free, but there is a fee to go into the tower, which is closed during Sunday service. The 240-foot tower offers a 360° view of the city, so it offers the best view and best place to take photos. http://en.hallgrimskirkja.is/.

Harpa Concert & Conference Center is another great landmark and a fairly new addition to the city. The award-winning center opened in 2011 and is considered to be one of the best concert halls in Northern Europe. Many music festivals are held here, as well as it being the home of the Iceland Symphony Orchestra. There is a gift shop, two restaurants, and guided tours are given daily. https://en.harpa.is/

Heidmork Nature Reserve is located just outside the city. It boasts twenty-six species of trees, with a total of more than four million trees. Additionally, there are thirty species of birds, lush vegetation, and many lava formations. There are numerous trails for hiking and exploring. http://www.visitreykjavik.is/heidmork-nature-reserve

Höfði House is another important building with an impressive history. It has been a meeting place for many monumental gatherings, such as the summit meeting of President Ronald Reagan and President Mikhail Gorbatsjov, which resulted in the end of the Cold War. The former home of the French Consul has welcomed other important visitors too, including the Queen of England and Winston Churchill. The house is reportedly haunted by the ghost known as "White Lady." At one time, this was the residence of the British Ambassador. But he was so plagued with ghostly activity, that he persisted the British Foreign Office sell the building. It is now owned by the city and is used for important events. The interior is not open to the public, but visitors are permitted to explore the grounds and take photos. http://www.visitreykjavik.is/hofdi-house

Iceland Expo Pavilion. This is a 360° cinematic experience that shares the best of Iceland. This unique and expensive attraction was created for the World's Fair in 2010. It is now located in Harpa where more than three million visitors have enjoyed seeing this short film. For fifteen thrilling minutes, participants will venture over erupting volcanos, through waterfalls, view wildlife up close, and go into the heart of Iceland. Shows are every thirty minutes, www.harpa.is.

Laugardalur Valley (also known as Hot Spring Valley) is a great resource for visitors. There is a campsite, youth hostel, Family Park & Zoo, botanical garden, Laugardalur Arena, art museum with sculpture garden, indoor ice skating rink, and largest outdoor thermal pool in Reykjavik. Swimming is permitted year round. The zoo features Icelandic animals, including arctic foxes, Viking horses, sheep, seals, and reindeer. There are lots of rides and a playground too. This is a romantic spot for couples, as well as a good place to go walking, cycling, and rollerblading. http://www.visitreykjavik.is/laugardalur-valley

Talk about a remote lighthouse!

FYI: Icelandair Hotel is leasing select lighthouses and renting them out seasonally, including Dyrahólaey Lighthouse and Garðskagaviti Lighthouse. You can have all the fun of being a lighthouse keeper without any of the work. Luckily, none are as remote as the Þrídrangar Lighthouse (pictured here) which is located six miles west of the Westman Islands on the highest of three rocks known as Háidrangur. Þrídrangar translates as "three rocks" in English. Can you imagine how hard this was to build?
http://icelandmonitor.mbl.is/news/nature_and_travel/2015/08/06/an_incredible_iceland_stopover/

For a list of all lighthouses in Iceland, including photos and details,
https://en.wikipedia.org/wiki/List_of_lighthouses_in_Iceland

Mount Esja is the best place near the city to hike. The 3,000-foot mountain has many well-posted trails with varying degrees of difficulty, but the view from anywhere on Mount Esja is the same—breathtaking. There is a guestbook to sign for those who make it all the way to the top. http://www.visitreykjavik.is/mount-esja

Nautholsvik Geothermal Beach. This manmade oasis opened in 2001 and draws more than 500,000 visitors annually. There is a beach and a lagoon enclosed by sea walls. In addition to soaking in the geothermal waters, visitors can also swim, sunbathe, sail, take a hot tub soak or a steam bath, and there are hot showers, toilets, and dressing rooms. Admission is free during summer months, but there is a fee in the winter. Refreshments can be purchased, and supplies may be rented. http://www.nautholsvik.is/desktopdefault.aspx/tabid-715/

FYI: Tjornin Pond, Old Harbor, and Oskjuhlid (wooded area around The Pearl) are all nice places to walk or relax. Snaefellsness Peninsula is a great place for photographers. It has fjords, volcanic peaks, sea cliffs, a beach, shark museum, and national park. See my TOP TEN PICKS for more about Ring Road and the Golden Circle. Also, don't forget there are dozens of nature, wildlife, and adventure tours you can take without venturing far from Reykjavik.

Sun Voyager (pictured here) is a large stainless steel sculpture created by artist John Gunnar Arnason. Most visitors like to have their photos taken standing beside the sculpture with Mount Esja in the background, especially at sunset. Sæbraut Road.

The Museum of Icelandic Sorcery & Witchcraft. At Strandagaldur, there is a museum catering to those fascinated with all things magical. The museum focuses on the elaborate and esoteric spells and rituals and contains a collection of Icelandic artifacts and displays such as runes and staves. There are some bizarre and disturbing displays and strange ingredients used to concoct certain Icelandic spells. http://www.galdrasyning.is/index.php?lang=en

The National Museum of Iceland shares the history and culture of Iceland. It has more than 2,000 pieces in its many exhibits. http://www.thjodminjasafn.is/english

The Pearl with City of Reykjavik in background

The Pearl is unmistakable. It is a huge, dome-shaped building, which is surrounded by six huge water tanks. It is home to a revolving restaurant, which is popular with tourists. The Pearl is also home to exhibits, special events, a café, and observation platform.
http://www.visitreykjavik.is/pearl

Þingvellir National Park (also known as Thingvellir) where you can find adorable Icelandic Horses. You'll also see sheep and can snorkel too! Þingvellir is a site of historical, cultural, and geological significance, and is one of the most popular tourist destinations in Iceland and a UNESCO World Heritage Site. The park, established in 1930, lies in a rift valley that marks the boundary between the North American tectonic plate and the Eurasian. To its south lies Þingvallavatn, the largest natural lake in Iceland. http://www.thingvellir.is/english.aspx

Reykjavik Art Museum is the largest art museum in Iceland, housed in three distinct buildings in central Reykjavik: Hafnarhús, Kjarvalsstaðir, and Ásmundarsafn. An admission ticket covers all three museums. The Reykjavík Art Museum hosts diverse cultural happenings, staging over a hundred events from lectures and seminars to unusual concerts. http://artmuseum.is/

Reykjavik City Museum includes five museums: Reykjavik Museum of Photography, Reykjavik Maritime Museum, Arbaer Open Air Museum (recreated Icelandic village), Settlement Exhibition, and Videy Island. http://reykjavik.is/en/museums

FYI: Phallological Museum is a one-of-a-kind museum with a collection of more than 282 phallic specimens. Philology is an ancient science and is taken seriously in the scientific world—or so I'm told. The museum displays penises of whales, polar bears, seals, walruses, and homo sapiens. In addition to the scientific specimens, there are also about 350 oddities and tools and related to the study of philology. The museum also displays works of art inspired by the penis. http://phallus.is/en/

Videy Island. Across the water from Reykjavik lies Videy Island. It was once the main harbor for the island until Reykjavik took over in 1943. These days, birds are the main inhabitants of the island with around thirty species coming here to breed. There is a restaurant, located in Videyjarstofa House, the first stone and cement building in Iceland, which dates from 1755. The island was once home to Augustine monks until 1539 when the Reformation began in Iceland. There is also a lovely church that is the oldest in Iceland and a house that was the first in the country to be built using stone. It can easily be explored on foot or by bike. It is best known for the Imagine Peace Tower. The tower was the brainchild of Yoko One as a symbol of world peace and in remembrance of John Lennon.

Laser light beams spell out IMAGINE PEACE in two dozen languages. The peace tower is well placed since Iceland has been ranked the most peaceful city in the world for eight years straight. The light tower shines from October to December to celebrate Lennon's birthday and commemorate his assassination date. Ferry service is free for Reykjavik City Card holders. http://www.visitreykjavik.is/videy-island

TERRANCE TALKS TRAVEL: The Quirky Tourist Guide to
Reykjavik | Terrance Zepke

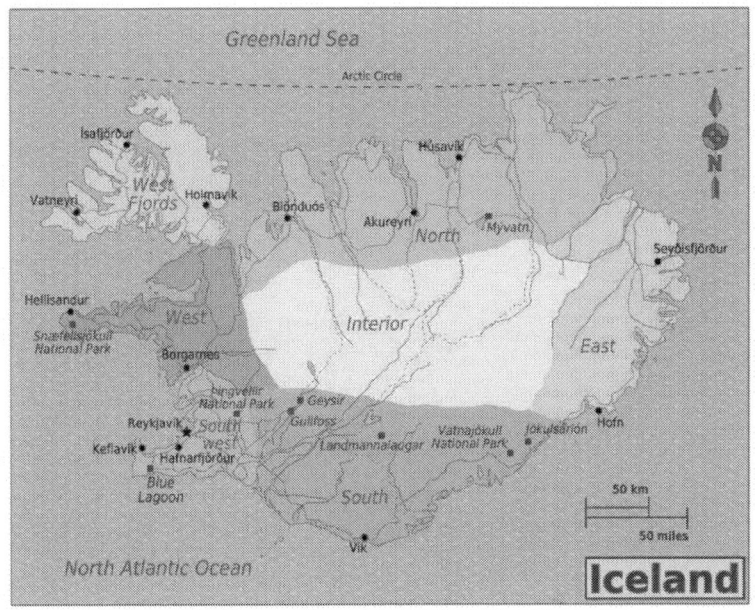

Adventure Tours

Just about any activity and tour is possible seasonally: glacier hiking, fishing, photography tours, horseback riding, jeep tours, hiking, city tours, glacier tours, snowmobile tours, ATV quad biking, whale watching, fishing, snorkeling, scuba diving, culture tours, paragliding, rafting, skiing, helicopter tours, and dog sledding. I have included a few favorites here, but you will find a comprehensive list on http://www.icelandtours.is/en and https://www.extremeiceland.is/en/activity-tours-iceland/

Aurora Borealis (a.k.a. Northern Lights) is a natural phenomenon that is a must see. This natural laser show is most often seen from November - February. There are scientific explanations for them, but they boring to those of us who have seen this spectacular sight If you're visiting in a different season when the lights can't be seen, don't worry. You can visit the Aurora Reykjavik and have the next best experience. This center offers exhibits and a presentation about the

Northern Lights. https://guidetoiceland.is/book-trips-holiday/nature-tours/northern-lights

Citywalk is a two-hour walking tour of Reykjavik. While it's not exactly adventurous, it is a popular tour. The guide shares history, folklore, and trivia about Iceland, including recommendations for food, music, and nightlife. The tour explores the oldest area of the city and reveals some fascinating facts. The best part is that it is free, but tips are encouraged. www.citywalk.is

Culture Tour with the colorful "Cultural Companion Birna" is quite the experience. Birna seems to know everyone in Reykjavik, and no one knows the downtown area better. She shares stories about its past and present and shows you the city from a cat's perspective. I told you it was an experience, didn't I? Participants will meander down alleys, little-known streets, and meet the locals. The tour lasts two hours. www.birna.is

Ice Cave Tour is an interesting option. Also known as Crystal Caves, ice caves are found inside glaciers. There are extensive cave systems in Vatnajokull (Southeast Iceland) and Langjokull (Southwest Iceland). https://www.extremeiceland.is/en/activity-tours-iceland/glacier-hiking-iceland/ice-caves

Puffin Tour takes you up close to these colorful, funny-looking birds. Participants are taken to Akurey and Lundey, which as Puffin hangouts. You transported by boat over to these islands. These tours are only offered April – August. https://elding.is/tours?type=puffin

Reykjavik Food Walk is a must for foodies. The tour takes you into downtown Reykjavik and includes thirteen local delicacies you most likely would not know about or have an opportunity to sample otherwise. This four-hour food lovers tour takes you to six restaurants, so be sure to bring your appetite. The tour operates once a day, Monday – Saturday. www.thereykjavikfoodwalk.com/

FYI: Vestmannaeyjar (also known as Westman Islands) is a town and archipelago off the south coast of Iceland. The largest island, Heimaey, has a population of 4,135. The other islands are uninhabited, although six have hunting cabins. Eldfell Volcano erupted in 1973, destroying a good portion of the town and causing the people to have to be evacuated for months. It took seven billion liters of sea water to stop the lava flow. Puffin tours and volcano tours are offered, as well as camping and a couple of restaurants.
www.visitwestmanislands.com

Your Friend in Reykjavik is to beer lovers what the Reykjavik Food Walk is to food lovers. Participants visit the city's best bars and sample ten craft beers that are only available in Iceland or northern Europe. They will share fun facts with you dating back to the Viking drinking days. *Skal!* (That means "Cheers!" in Icelandic, and you'll be saying that at least ten times during the tour). They offer a Viking Tour that sounds fun. http://www.yourfriendinreykjavik.com/ourtours/

FYI: Did you know there are sixty-five golf courses in Iceland? http://www.worldgolf.com/courses/iceland/.

The biggest annual golf event is the Arctic Open. This is a 36-hole tournament, played at Akureyri Golf Club on the north end of the island that goes well past midnight because of the summer's Midnight Sun. www.arcticopen.is.

There are so many activities that most folks don't know about in greater Reykjavik, including whale watching, ice cave tours, helicopter tours, reindeer safaris, Viking horse tours, snorkeling, Northern Lights viewing cruise, snowmobiling, hiking glaciers, and much more.
For a complete list of options, visit https://www.viator.com/Iceland/d55-ttd?pref=204, http://www.tour.is/info/adventure-tours.php, https://www.icelandtravel.is/day-tours/#/?rows=18&q=&sort=sort_i%20desc, or www.visiticeland.com.

BEST OF REYKJAVIK

Reykjavik is chock full of cafes, bistros, bars, clubs, and restaurants. Some Europeans make a stopover on route home to spend a night or two in Reykjavik. To be honest, there are so many fun night spots and good restaurants that it was often hard to narrow it down to one "BEST" place. For a comprehensive list of establishments, visit https://guidetoiceland.is/.

BEST BREWERY: Olgerdin Brewery. Established in 1913, this is the oldest brewery in Iceland. Visitors can take a tour of the facility and taste samples, as well as order from an extensive menu of alcoholic beverages.
http://www.olgerdin.is/en

FYI: Alcohol was prohibited in Iceland during the early 1900s, and beer was banned until 1989. A creative beer substitute, Brennivin, was concocted and can still be sampled at some bars. It is distilled from potatoes and caraway seeds, so it has a strange flavor and strong aftertaste. Believe me, it does not taste like any beer you've ever consumed!

BEST PLACE TO SEE SUNSET: During the summer months, the **west coast of Iceland** is the perfect place to witness the setting of the midnight sun. The sun doesn't set until very late during Iceland's summer months, but it is a sight worth waiting to see!

BEST GEYSER: Strokkur Geyser erupts every few minutes, just like "Old Faithful" in Yellowstone National Park. Iceland is one of only four countries in the world where you can see hydrogeological geysers. This geyser became active in 1789 when an earthquake occurred and has been erupting ever since. Be sure to stand back as the water from geysers averages 210°F (100°C)!

BEST GLACIER: Vatnajokull Glacier is the biggest and best in Europe. It is part of Vatnajokull National Park and comprises eight percent of Iceland.

BEST GEOTHERMAL SPA: Blue Lagoon. The lagoon is a man-made lagoon which is fed by the water output of the nearby geothermal power plant Svartsengi and is renewed every two days. Superheated water is vented from the ground near a lava flow and used to run turbines that generate electricity. After going through the turbines, the steam and hot water passes through a heat exchanger to provide heat for a municipal water heating system. Then the water is fed into the lagoon. It is one of the top twenty-five wonders of the world. http://www.bluelagoon.com/

BEST WATERFALL: Seljalandsfoss Waterfall (pictured here) is 213 feet and absolutely stunning from the front or back. There is a trail leading into a cave so that you can walk "into" the waterfall from the backside. Be sure to bring a raincoat if you want to have a close-up experience. **Runner Up: Skogafoss Waterfall**

BEST PLACE FOR COFFEE: Famous Illy offers gourmet coffee, delicious homemade goodies, and serves breakfast and lunch. www.facebook.com/cookie.reykjavik

BEST PLACE FOR TEA: **Te & Kaffi** opened its doors in 1984. They offer a fine selection of exotic teas and tea-related gifts. They also serve good coffee. www.teogkaffi.is

FYI: You can find Coca Cola® everywhere. That's because more Coke is consumed per capita than anywhere else in the world.

BEST PLACE FOR A STEAK: Argentina Steakhouse dates back to 1989. They specialize in quality steaks and fish, grilled Argentinean style. www.en.argentina.is

BEST PLACE FOR LOBSTER: Not surprisingly, it is a place with the word "lobster" in it. The **Lobster House** is my favorite Reykjavik restaurant. Many of the locals feel the same way. It has a nice ambiance and great food.

Address: Amtmannsstígur 1

BEST PLACE TO HAVE A DRINK: Saemundur. This is a gastro pub in KEX hostel. Its menu changes daily but the drink menu remains the same. This place has a cool atmosphere and good vibe for savoring a cold cocktail, beer, or premium wine at happy hour or late night. This hip and happening place often has entertainment, such as a comedy act, karaoke, open mic night, or musical concerts. www.kexhostel.is.

Runner Up: **Micro Bar** in Center Hotel.

BEST PLACE FOR PIZZA: Gamla Smidjan creates the best pizzas in Reykjavík. We're talking traditional and some rather inventive concoctions! www.gamlasmidjan.is

BEST PLACE TO GRAB A BEER, READ A BOOK, & WASH A LOAD: Laundromat Café. You can do it all here: wash a load of laundry, read one of their 5,000 books, browse a magazine or newspaper, play a board game, grab a beer or coffee, and have a good meal. They are renowned for their Sunday brunch and pot roast. www.laundromatcafe.com

BEST PLACE FOR BRUNCH: Kaffivagninn. This rather looks like a hole in the wall, but this old fisherman's café serves simple but delicious meals. Located by the old harbor, the view is great too. Address: Grandagardur 10

BEST HOT DOG: Hands down, it is the **Baejarins Beztu Pylsur (a.k.a. The Town's Best) Hot Dog Stand**, located at the harbor. Be prepared for a long line, especially on weekends, as everyone knows it's the best place to grab a dog. Even former U.S. President Bill Clinton has dined here. First timers should grab plenty of napkins and try the "Classic," which comes with remoulade, mustard, ketchup, and lots of onions. www.bbp.is/

 **FYI: Bæjarins Beztu Pylsur, is more than one hot dog hut.** It is a chain of hot dog stands located in Reykjavík. Baujarins Beztu has been in continuous operation since 1937 when the first stand was set up. In the 1960s, it moved to Tryggvagata, across from the Harpa Concert Hall, and is considered to be the main stand in the chain.

BEST PLACE FOR A BURGER: **Hamborgarafabrikkan** (a.k.a. The Hamburger Factory). Say that three times fast! Choose from fourteen specialty burgers, all made with high-quality meat and the best ingredients. A local favorite is a lamburger. www.hamborgaragabrikkan.is

BEST PLACE FOR APPETIZERS: **Forréttabarinn** features creative and tasty starters (or sample several instead of dinner!) and is located at the Old Harbor. forrettabarinn@forrettabarinn.is

BEST BAKERY: Café Konditori Copenhagen specializes in Icelandic bread, cookies, and cakes. Yum! Address: Grensavegur 26.

FYI: If you're going to be in Reykjavik on a weekend, you are in for a treat. Every weekend, many take to the streets to participate in "RÚNTUR." This is one big bar crawl on Laugavegur. But you better take a nap as this is a test of endurance! Most residents start drinking at home and don't hit the streets until midnight. They usually carry on until 5 a.m. when they grab takeaway (we call it food to go in the States) and head home. It is loud and long, but never too raucous!

BEST BISTRO: Geysir Bistro & Bar is a trendy bistro inside the Tourist Information

Centre. Here you can use their Wi-Fi to catch up on emails, news, and sports scores, as well as grab lunch or dinner. Their specialty is fish and meat dishes, which will satisfy even the heartiest appetite. They also serve salads and soup for those seeking a lighter fare. www.geysirbistroybar.is.

BEST ICELANDIC FOOD & BEST VIEW: Café Loki. This is probably my second favorite restaurant. It is cozy, and the food and service are excellent. I highly recommend their homemade soups and breads, Icelandic plate, and dessert cakes. The restaurant looks out over the city with a keen view of Hallgrimskirkja and the Blafjoll mountains. www.loki.is

BEST IRISH PUB: The Dubliner is the oldest established Irish pub in Iceland. www.dubliner.is.

BEST ENGLISH PUB: The English Pub serves forty brands of beer, ale, and whiskey. It is a classic English pub. www.enskibarinn.is/

BEST PLACE FOR LIVE MUSIC: Café Rosenberg is a jazz joint in downtown Reykjavik. They offer live music nightly, although not always jazz. The inside resembles a quintessential jazz club. www.caferosenberg.is

BEST NIGHTCLUB: Austur. It remains the hottest club in town since first opening its doors in 2009. This modern nightclub has just the right atmosphere and energy for those looking to dance and have a good time. www.facebook.com/austurclub

FYI: Reykjavik Bar Rules: *The Rules Are They Are No Rules!* **Well, almost. There is no such thing as a cover charge unless it is a special event. There is no dress code. Most places offer Happy Hour specials. The legal drinking age is 20, but some bars have an age minimum of 21 or older. Most bars close at 1 a.m. on weeknights and close as late as 5 a.m. on weekends.**

BEST THEME RESTAURANT: Fjorugardurinn. What's the theme? Viking, Viking, and more Viking! The décor is Viking, the food is Viking, and the experience is 100% Viking. It is open for dinner only, and there is also live music and dancing on the weekend. Be forewarned! The waiters and waitresses also double as singing Valkyries and Vikings! It will be a night to remember. www.fjorukrain.is

BEST COZY BAR: Kofi Tomasar Franenda is a cozy, basement café. It is a good place to stop in and take a short break while sightseeing or shopping. They are in the heart of the city and serve light refreshments all day and night. On the weekend, they have music, and a DJ so get there by 11:30 p.m. if you want a table. www.facebook.com/kofinn.ktf

BEST FUNKY BAR: Barinn (formerly Club 22). There are three floors of entertainment with décor and music varying according to location, so there is something for everyone. The dining area is on the main level. It is funky and fun and a must for the quirky traveler. **Runner UP: Kaffibarinn.**

https://www.facebook.com/kaffibarinn

BEST SPORTS BAR: Players is a classic sports bar where one can watch sports and play a game of pool. They also serve food, and on weekends there is dancing. Address: Baejarlind 4

BEST UPSCALE BAR: B5 is as sophisticated as it gets with a strict dress code enforced and two VIP lounges. http://b5.is/

BEST VEGETARIAN RESTAURANT: Glo is an award-winning eatery with all ingredients being organic and fresh, sourced as much as possible from Icelandic farmers. www.glo.is/glorestauranticeland.

BEST GROOVY BAR: For those with a more sophisticated scene (think blues and Pinot Gris), **Café Rosenberg** is your place. www.facebook.com/pages/Caf%C3%A9-Rosenberg/235965816459522.

BEST LGBT BAR: Q Bar has a DJ nightly and live music on weekends. Address: Ingólfsstræti 3.

BEST SHOPPING: The main streets of **Laugavegur, Austurstraeti, Laekjargata** and **Skolavordustigur,** are all located in the center of Reykjavik. If you're looking for outdoor clothing or Icelandic design, check out Spaks, Kraum, Kisan and Jör. The **Reykjavik Flea Market** is held on the weekends. This is where you can find lots of food vendors and bargains, such hand-knitted wool sweaters and jackets. Also, on the outskirts of town is the Alafoss Factory Store. The city mall is Kringlan, and there is a large mall, Smáralind, in the Kópavogur suburb.

BEST PLACES FOR SOUVENIRS:

*Dogma for souvenir t-shirts.

*12 Tonar for music.

*Blue Lagoon gift shop for beauty products.

*National Museum of Iceland gift shop for kitsch souvenirs (fridge magnets, Viking dolls, plush puffins, etc.)

*66° North gear and Kisan for brand name clothing and Icelandic woolen goods.

*Aurum for jewelry.

*Any liquor store to buy Reyka Vodka.

COOLEST BAR: *Literally!* **Kaffi Reykjavik Ice Bar** is the coolest bar in town because its walls, tables, bar, and glasses are all constructed from Icelandic glaciers, and the interior stays at -6°c year round. You will receive an insulated coat and gloves to wear during your visit and a complimentary vodka cocktail. This place is so cool that it is the hottest place in town! I haven't been to this place, but I have done the Ice Bar elsewhere, and it is a memorable experience and a must for quirky travelers! Address: Vesturgata 2

BEST PLACE TO GET A COCKTAIL: Most bars and cafes in Iceland cater to a beer and wine crowd. If you're looking for a martini or cosmopolitan, you need to go to **Hotel Holt's Gallery Bar**. Not only are the drinks better than anywhere else in town, but the atmosphere is also more sophisticated. The bar is lined with paintings done by some by some of the best artists in Iceland, and you will enjoy the comfort of their buttery soft leather club chairs. http://www.holt.is/english/drink/gallery-bar/.

Runner Up: Slippbarrin in the Reykjavik Hotel Marina.

BEST BOOKSTORE: Ida Zimsen. This quaint bookstore sells books and goodies. You can grab a cup of coffee (or latte or hot chocolate), one of their famous muffins or cookies, and browse through their book collection. https://www.facebook.com/IdaZimsen

BEST SPA FOR THE ADVENTUROUS: Fish Ice Spa in downtown Reykjavik uses unconventional treatments (not allowed in the U.S.), including using Garra Rufa Fish to eliminate dead skin. http://www.fishspa.is/.

FYI: The Garra Rufa fish have no teeth, and therefore they do not bite and do not hurt, but massage, removing the hard shell of skin from your feet and hands. It makes your skin softer, prettier and healthier. The Garra Rufa fish is successful in finding the nerve endings, which helps in establishing the balance of the nervous system, relax the whole body and the general feeling of well-being.

ABOUT ACCOMMODATIONS

Rentals

There are a surprising number of options, including many houses, guesthouses, and apartment rentals. To find a **vacation rental**, I recommend using www.airbnb.com, www.rent.is, and www.booking.com and searching "Iceland" to find all listings. Also, www.accommodation.is has a user-friendly search engine that lists accommodations by location.

BEST GUESTHOUSE: Three Sisters. This nicely renovated apartment guesthouse offers sixteen fully-equipped studio apartments. It is located on a quiet street within easy walking distance of the heart of the city and its main shopping district. www.threesisters.is

Best APARTMENT: Grettisborg Apartments are six new self-catering apartments in one of the best locations in the city. Units can accommodate one couple with four children or four adults. www.grettisborg.is/

Hotels

Here are some **hotel** recommendations. To see photos, prices, and all listings, visit www.stay.com/reykjavik/hotel/, www.hotels.is, www.Reykjavikcenter.is, and www.visiticeland.com.

BEST LUXURY HOTEL: Grand Hotel Reykjavik is centrally-located with conference facilities, guest rooms and suites, and first class amenities. http://en.grand.is/

Runner Up: Radisson BLU 1919 Hotel is one of the city's most historical buildings. This property has also won many awards for service. www.radissonblu.com/1919hotel-reykjavik

Best HIPSTER HOTEL: Canopy Reykjavik offers complimentary artisanal buffet breakfast (or for early tours you can have their Canopy Break Fast To Go Bag) and evening refreshments are served in their on-site restaurant. Their Just Right Rooms are painted and decorated in hues of ocean blue and volcanic gray. All rooms have Nespresso coffee makers, large screen TVs, mini-fridges, and super comfy beds. Wi-Fi is free for all guests, and there are bikes for getting around the city and a fitness center.
www.canopyreykjavik.canopybyhilton.com

Hostels

There are two dozen hostels in Iceland and many are on par with guesthouses and farm stays. Some have private rooms and dorms with meal service, and all have guest kitchens and self-service laundry. It is important to note that hostels fill up faster than hotels and guesthouses in high season, so you need to plan ahead. Some hostels are closed during the winter. All ages are welcome, including older travelers and children. www.hostel.is and www.hihostels.com

BEST HOSTEL: Kex Hostel is a cozy, conveniently-located, and affordable place to stay. It offers dorms, family rooms, and private rooms, free Wi-Fi, a gastro pub (Saemundur), and a bar, DRINX. www.kexhostel.is

Runner Up: Reykjavik Downtown Hostel is at

the harbor, which is in the heart of the city's action. It offers free Wi-Fi, book exchange, self-service kitchen, lounge, coffee bar, and more. It has been environmentally eco-certified since 2010. www.hostel.is/hostels/reykjavikdowntown

Farm stays

A farm stay is simply a guesthouse in farm surroundings that is on par with those of a European bed-and-breakfast.

BEST FARMSTAY: Hey Iceland has 150 "farmhouses," "cottages," and "country hotels" throughout Iceland. All of their options include private bathrooms and meals or use of a guest kitchen. Some have amenities, such as hot tubs and horseback riding. www.farmholidays.is.

Camping

There are more than two dozen campsites scattered throughout Iceland. They are all safe, nice, and conveniently located (almost every village has one). There is even a campsite in Reykjavik. www.reykjavikcampsite.is. Most camp sites have hot showers, toilets, electricity, laundry facilities, and kitchens. Camping is popular with Icelanders, so these sites book up fast during the high season, which is summer. Most campsites are only open during the summer months. It is best to get a **Camping Card**, which gives a couple or family access to all campgrounds for a prolonged period of time. Some national park campsites are not included. www.campingcard.is. A comprehensive list of campsites can be found on www.camping.is.

FYI: Reykjavik which was recently named UNESCO World City of Literature. The city was recognized for its strong presence of writers, poets and children's book authors who give it a unique position in the world of literature. Iceland's unique environment is matched by its distinctive folklore which is rich in tales of aquatic monsters, ghosts, spirits, elves and trolls. During the long dark nights of Icelandic winters, storytelling was the chief form of entertainment with each region having its own colorful legends passed down over the centuries through oral and written traditions. Elves and trolls play an integral role in Icelandic folklore. Visitors to Iceland can learn about elves in Hafnarfjordur, a town just outside Reykjavik that has special tours, an elf spotting map and a dedicated school offering a real elfin education complete with a diploma.

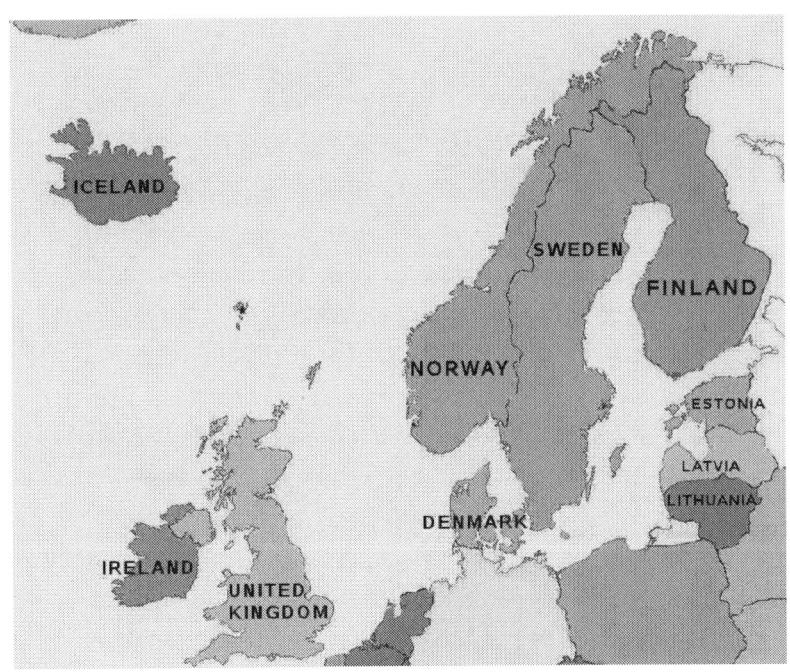

ABOUT ICELAND

The Republic of Iceland is the most sparsely populated country in Europe. This Nordic island nation is volcanically and geologically active.

There are forty volcanoes on this island. One erupts every five years on average.

Its high latitude and location in the North Atlantic Ocean cause summers to be cool and creates a tundra climate. Iceland is due east of Greenland and abuts the Arctic Circle. It is north of just about everywhere in the world and quite remote. So is it the journey or the destination? I think in this case, travelers get rewarded with both. It is an incredible journey for most of us to reach this part of the world, and once there travelers discover how remarkable Iceland truly is. This small island nation has a lot to offer!

Nearly fifteen percent of the country is covered by glaciers and snowfields. The largest glacier in Europe is Iceland's Hvannadalshnukur, which is a 6,500-foot peak. The largest geyser is Europe is here. They have more geothermal pools than anywhere else in the world. The coastline boasts more than 100 fjords and the interior has more than 10,000 waterfalls and too many hot springs to count.

Iceland is roughly the size of the state of Kentucky with both having a land mass of 40,000 square miles. It has a population of approximately 333,000. Most of its inhabitants live in and around the capital city of Reykjavik.

The first permanent settler was Ingolfur Arnarson, a Norwegian who arrived in 874 A.D. The earliest inhabitants of this Nordic country were Irish hermits, who left when the pagan Norse people arrived in the latter part of the 9th century. During the mid-1200s, Iceland came under Norwegian rule and passed into Danish control when the kingdoms of Norway, Sweden, and Denmark were unified in 1397.

By 1874, Iceland got its own constitution. Even though Denmark recognized Iceland as a sovereign nation, it remained under Danish rule until 1944 when it was finally declared an independent republic following the war.

Today, Iceland's economy is dependent on tourism and fisheries. Three-fourths of all exports are seafood products. And tourism is growing exponentially as more and more travelers discover all that Iceland has to offer. Many airlines now fly into Iceland daily, and numerous tour operators offer a variety of tour packages.

Here is a helpful timeline of significant events in Iceland history:

7-8th centuries: Celtic monks sail to Iceland.

860s: Norsemen discover Iceland.

871: Ingólfur Arnarsson, a Norse nobleman, settles in Reykjavík.

930: The Althing, a judiciary and law-making body of chieftains, convenes for the first time at Thingvellir. Population in Iceland estimated at 30,000–40,000.

982: Erik the Red discovers and names Greenland after being banned from Iceland.

999 or 1000: Christianity adopted in Iceland.

1000: Leifur Eriksson discovers what is now known as North America.

The 1120s–1230s: Most of the Icelandic Sagas—tales of family feuds and heroics—are written.

1262–1264: Chieftains in Iceland accept the sovereignty of the King of Norway.

1402: The Black Plague infects Iceland. Over 33% of the population is wiped out.

1387: The Kalmar Act of Union unifies Iceland and

Norway with Denmark.

The 1540s–1550s: Reformation in Iceland.

1584: The Bible is translated into Icelandic.

1703: First census is conducted; population 50,358.

1707: Bubonic plague; one-third of the population dies.

1783–86: Volcanic activity destroys Icelandic farmland and leads to widespread starvation.

1800: The Danish King orders the closure of the Althing.

1843: The Althing is re-established.

1874: A new constitution is introduced by the Danish King (Christian IX).

The 1870s–1890s: Mass emigration to North America.

1904: Home rule is granted.

1915: Women receive the vote.

1918: Union Treaty grants Iceland full sovereignty in a royal union with Denmark.

1926: Population reaches 100,000 for the first time.

1940: Iceland is occupied by British troops.

1941: US-Icelandic defense agreement signed; US troops stay in Iceland for the duration of WWII.

1944: The Republic of Iceland is formally established.

1949: Iceland becomes a founding member of NATO.

1951: Defense treaty concluded with the US; US troops return to Iceland.

1958–1961: Dispute over fishing limits, first 'cod war' with Britain.

1960: The number of Icelanders in Reykjavík and surrounding areas surpasses the number of inhabitants in the countryside for the first time.

1966: Icelandic state television begins broadcasting.

1968: Population reaches 200,000.

The 1970s: Two further 'cod wars' with Britain (and West Germany).

1980: Vigdís Finnbogadóttir elected president, the first democratically-elected female head of state.

1986: The Reykjavík Summit between US President Ronald Reagan and Soviet Secretary-General of the Communist Party, Mikhail Gorbachev takes place in Höfði, Reykjavík.

1994: Iceland joins the European Economic Area, an economic arrangement with the EU.

1996: Ólafur Ragnar Grímsson elected president of Iceland

2006: US troops leave Iceland.

2008: Economic crisis, near total collapse of Iceland's banking system.

2009: Jóhanna Sigurdardóttir becomes the country's first female prime minister (and the world's first openly gay

prime minister).
2010: Volcanic Eruption at the Eyjafjallajökull. This same year Jón Gnarr, a known actor, and comedian in Iceland became mayor of Reykjavik (2010-2014).
2015: Residents in Iceland number 329.100. Icelandic citizens 296,700.

FYI: In late March 2010, the Eyjafjallajokull Volcano erupted. The event produced minimal seismic activity but resulted in an enormous volcanic ash plume that lingered for a long time over northern and central Europe.

ANNUAL EVENTS & AVERAGE TEMPS

Iceland has many different annual events which attract travelers from all over the world each year. Here is a summary:

Thorrablot / Þorrablót (Mid-January to mid-February) This ancient Viking midwinter tradition was originally a feast of sacrifice to the Norse God Thor and is celebrated today with plenty of dancing, singing, and feasting on traditional Viking foods like boiled sheep's head and fermented shark washed down with Brennivin, the local caraway-seed flavored spirit fondly known as 'black death.' Modern day Icelanders don't normally eat these foods, but during the month of Thor, the traditional 'delicacies' fill grocery store shelves and restaurants offer special Thorrablot menus. Festivities vary from informal dinners with family and friends to large organized events with entertainment and activities.

Winter Lights Festival (Mid to late February) Reykjavik is cheerfully lit up for this celebration of cultural events dedicated to the theme of energy and light. Events include ice skating exhibitions to outdoor choral performances.

Reykjavik Food & Fun Festival (Late Feb to early Mar) Promotions at restaurants throughout Reykjavik bring to light the achievements of chefs and manufacturers of Icelandic gourmet products such as caviar, shrimp, lamb, and cheese. Internationally renowned chefs visit the capital and are paired with a restaurant to create a special menu for the week at discounted prices.

Reykjavik Fashion Festival & Design March (Mid-March) Started in 2010; the Reykjavik Fashion Festival provides an arena for new Icelandic designers to showcase their clothing lines and fully express their visions in a cutting-edge event program where avant-garde fashion, music and fun fuse together seamlessly for all to enjoy. Design March presents exhibitions, workshops and events across the city from the world of design ranging from architecture to fashion, fonts, furniture and food.

Cream Puff Day / Bolludagur (February-March) Two days before Lent Iceland celebrates 'Cream Puff Day' or Bolludagur when homes, restaurants, and bakeries overflow with delicately made cream puffs in all different shapes and sizes, filled with cream, jam, and sometimes drizzled in chocolate. Children wake their parents early from bed with a colorfully decorated Bolluvondur wand and receive a cream puff for each whack of the wand they can land.

Shrove Tuesday / Sprengidagur (February-March) The day before Lent is known as Sprengidagur or 'Bursting Day' when every Icelandic home and most restaurants flood with the aroma of Saltkjot & baunir or salted lamb meat and peas, a traditional stew-like meal. The name 'Sprengidagur' refers to the idea that individuals feast on this hearty dish to the point of bursting.

Ash Wednesday / Oskudagur (February-March) Ash Wednesday is celebrated in Iceland with a unique custom for children. Ashes are collected into small bags known as 'Oskupokar.' As a prank, these bags are secretly pinned onto people's clothing. The day is also marked with children singing and parading around the streets and shops, begging for treats.

Easter (Late March - April)
On Easter Sunday the traditional meal of roasted Icelandic lamb is served with rhubarb jelly and sugar-browned potatoes. Children and grown-ups alike enjoy hollowed-out chocolate Easter eggs filled with candy treats and a Malshatt which is a tiny piece if Icelandic wisdom originating from some 400 proverbs based on folklore, history, and homilies. Easter Monday is also an official holiday in Iceland commonly celebrated by families getting together for outdoor fun and relaxation. The Thursday and Friday before Easter are also official holidays.

First Day of Summer (3rd Thursday in April)
According to ancient Icelandic calendars, summer starts early, and modern-day Icelanders celebrate this national holiday with colorful parades, street entertainment, and sporting events.

Reykjavik Arts Festival (Late May)
This two-week cultural festival showcases a wide array of concerts, operas, dance and theater

performances at local venues including the National Gallery, Harpa and the Nordica House with spin-off events throughout the country.

Festival of the Sea / Sjomannadagur (1st weekend in June)

This holiday runs the first weekend of June and pays tribute to those who make their living by the sea with colorful parades, cultural celebrations, seafood fairs and fisherman rescue demonstrations, rowing races, and strongman competitions.

Viking Festival (Mid-June)

Modern day Vikings from across the globe descend upon the quaint town of Hafnarfjordur just outside Reykjavik for a weekend of lively festivities in period costume, traditional crafts and staged battles.

Icelandic Independence Day (June 17)

Iceland declared independence from Danish rule in 1944 and is celebrated on June 17th because it was the birthday of Jon Sigurdsson who is regarded as Iceland's champion to the nationalist cause. After morning ceremonies in downtown Reykjavik, afternoon crowds gather around the country for vibrant parades, traditional dancing, street performers, and theatrical entertainment.

Summer Solstice (Jun 21)
Celebrations around Reykjavik honor the magic of the Midnight Sun on the longest day of the year when many Icelanders gather late at night to watch the sun dip below the horizon and rise back up again shortly afterward.

Arctic Open International Golf Tournament (Late June) Held just south of the Arctic Circle in the picturesque town of Akureyri; the Arctic Open is a four-day championship golfing tournament open to professionals and amateurs alike. Tee off at midnight in bright sunshine and play through the night in a distinctive natural setting.

Gay Pride Parade (2nd weekend in August)
There are several fun activities throughout Reykjavik which is decorated with rainbows as thousands of people gather to watch the highly anticipated Gay Pride Parade.

Reykjavik Culture Night / Menningarnott (3rd weekend in August) On this enchanted evening downtown Reykjavik is closed to traffic, and the city center transforms into a cultural mecca of free exhibitions, concerts, poetry readings, and street theater with every venue in the city utilized. Choice selections of food and drink are served, and the evening is concluded with a fireworks display over Tjornin Pond.

Reykjavik Marathon (3rd weekend in August) The Reykjavik Marathon is an annual event held every August on Culture Day. This international event hosts over 3,500 participants for a full or half marathon, or three, five or ten-kilometer races as well as an informal family races.

Labor Day Weekend / Verslunnarmannahelgi (1st weekend in August) The first weekend in August is a three-day holiday with everything closed on Monday. Most Icelanders head out of the city to camp in the wild or join in one of the organized events that are held throughout this country. The most popular location is the Westman Islands, where thousands of visitors gather at the campground to hear live bands and party around the bonfires into the wee morning hours.

Sheep and Horse Round-Up (Early September)

September brings the farming tradition of Rettir, an entertaining and interesting process where farmers set off on horseback to gather their sheep and horses that have spent the summer grazing in the highlands. Once the flocks are penned and sorted by their earmarks, the farming communities host spirited celebrations with singing, dancing, and drinking into the night. Visitors are welcome to participate, and it is an ideal time to explore Iceland's backcountry during the colorful fall season.

Imagine Peace Tower (October 9 – December 8)

In 2007 Yoko Ono unveiled the Imagine Peace Tower, a beam of light emanating from a wishing well monument on the coast of Videy Island just outside of Reykjavik. Created in memory of her husband, John Lennon, it bears the words Imagine Peace in 24 languages & is lit each year from Oct 9 - Dec 8.

Iceland Airwaves Music Festival (Early November)

This highly anticipated five-day alternative/indie musical showcase attracts thousands of music lovers from around the world to check out Icelandic and international talent at various venues across the vibrant capital of Reykjavik during Northern Lights season.

Reykjavik International Film Festival / RIFF (Late September-early October)

This 10-day event features a selection of the year's best in world cinema and includes film classics, premiers, retrospectives, seminars, and workshops.

Reykjavik Jazz Festival (Late August)

The Reykjavik Jazz Festival boasts a stellar line-up of jazz and blues artists from around the world playing a variety of styles at local clubs and venues during the last two weeks of August.

FYI: Christmas traditions and activities abound in Iceland. There are special seasonal events and tours to celebrate Christmas, including a Reykjavik Christmas Special and New Year's Day Dinner Cruise. See below for a partial list, but for all activities, https://www.icelandtravel.is/christmas-and-new-year/#/?rows=18&q=&sort=sort_i%20desc

Christmas Season (December)

When the days are short, beloved Icelandic Christmas folklore adds to the mystique of the holidays with tales of 13 Yuletide lads, their troll mother Gryla and a killer Christmas cat. City streets around the country twinkle in festive lighting, towns set up their outdoor Christmas markets and restaurants put forward scrumptious smorgasbords. Family celebrations begin on December 24th when many people attend mass before going to a festive dinner, exchanging gifts and dancing around the Christmas tree.

FYI: Every country has a different Christmas traditions. Instead of Santa Claus, Icelanders have Yule Lads. They are descendants of trolls and have colorful names, costumes, and personalities. There come during Advent, one each day, to bring a gift to small children.

Happy New Year!

New Year's Eve (December 31)
New Year's Eve in Iceland is a spectacular celebration that has to be seen to be believed. Nowhere in the world are more fireworks used on this holiday, when private use of fireworks is legal for this one night only, and the entire country sets the skies ablaze in celebration.

Christmas Markets

There are a couple of Christmas markets in Reykjavik that lasts throughout the month of December: Yule Town and Jólakrás Street Food Christmas Market. Yule Town includes ice skating, food vendors, handicrafts and decorations for sale, and more. The Jolakras Market is all about Christmas-themed street food. Yum! Just outside of the city is the Heidmark Christmas Market and Christmas Tree Sale. This is open weekends from late November until Christmas. There are concerts and storytelling, as well as food and handmade Christmas items.

A Christmas Village is set up in downtown Hafnarfjordur during the Advent season. Highlights include a best snowman contest, entertainment, food vendors, and hand-crafted items for sale. This is open late November until Christmas.

FYI: The Children's Christmas Workshop opens in Reykjavík City Hall in early December and runs until the end of the first week of January. At the workshop, families can create Christmas decorations, and explore the Christmas Cave.

Just for fun...

Icelanders are quite traditional when it comes to their Christmas food. Many recipes have been handed down for generations. Here are some traditional foods:

Hangikjöt is the smoked lamb traditionally served by Icelanders over the Christmas holidays. The meat is usually served with potatoes in Béchamel sauce and green peas, but there are several other imaginative ways to make a meal of this delicious local delicacy. Leftover Hangikjöt can be used on Icelandic flatbread, in sandwiches or as a tasty snack. Hangikjöt is usually boiled, but each family will have its own opinion on how to boil it and for how long. Try it with the Christmas favorite Malt & Appelsín, a mix of two soft drinks that has become traditional.

Many households will serve **Ptarmigan** on Christmas Eve. Ptarmigan is a bird in the grouse family and has a similarly gamey taste. Like with the Hangikjöt, each family will have their own way of preparing and serving the ptarmigan. However, most people will serve it with caramelized potatoes and pickled red cabbage. AT one time, ptarmigan was eaten in poorer households, ones that couldn't afford lamb, but today the dish has become very popular and sometimes the meat is even sold out in shops.

Smoked ham is usually the alternative to Hangikjöt. The custom is originally Danish but has been a part of the Icelandic Christmas for many years. The ham is glazed with mustard and brown sugar and served with caramelized potatoes, red cabbage and brown sauce. Similar to Hangikjöt, the leftover ham is often served on Icelandic flatbread at family gatherings after the holidays.

Skate is a fish closely related to the species of rays. Skate is considered a delicacy in Iceland and is served on Thorlak's Mass on December 23rd. The skate is putrefied and therefore has a very strong smell. On Thorlak's Mass wherever you are, you are sure to run into the smell before you hear the noise of Icelander's making merry.

Skate is usually served with boiled potatoes and rye bread.

What most Icelanders find essential to Christmas is the **Leaf Bread**. Ingredients to make the wafer thin bread were hard to find most times of the year except around Christmas, and the bread was baked so thin so everyone could have a piece. Decorative patterns are carved into the bread to make it more festive.

A tradition that originates in Denmark, the cold rice pudding known as **Risalamande** has become a crucial part of the Christmas meal for many Icelanders. Rice is boiled in milk and vanilla, and after it has cooled, cream and almonds are mixed in. It is then served as a dessert on Christmas Eve with either cherry- or applesauce. Many families will play a game where a whole almond is hidden in the pudding and the one who finds it wins a small prize.

Icelandic horses were brought to Iceland by the Vikings around 900 A.D. They are a hardy and friendly breed.

FYI: There are thousands of whales and porpoises in the surrounding North Atlantic Ocean. Seals can also be seen along the shorelines in Reykjavik or sitting atop a blue iceberg floating in the Jokulsarlon glacial lagoon. There are 300 species of birds throughout the island, as well as sheep and Icelandic horses. Wild reindeer can be found roaming the countryside in the East.

Although all these creatures now call Iceland home, it is believed that the Arctic Fox is the only indigenous animal.

Average Temps

The Gulf Stream brings mild Atlantic air in contact with colder Arctic air, resulting in frequent and abrupt weather shifts where you may experience four seasons in one day. The Icelanders often say, *"If you don't like the weather, just wait fifteen minutes, and you'll get something different."*

Iceland does not have a rainy season, but precipitation peaks in October to February, with the southern and western parts receiving the most rainfall. The North, East and Interior experience colder winter temperatures but warmer summers, and noticeably less snow and rain. Iceland's most influencing weather element is the wind. The Icelandic language describes at least eight different degrees of wind, from logn (calm breeze) to rok (strong gale). Although Iceland is located just south of the Arctic Circle, it does have four distinct seasons:

Winters are mild with the average January temperature in Reykjavik (-0.5°C /31°F) similar to New York City or Hamburg. It is not unusual to see snow in October or April, but it rarely stays on the ground for more than a few days. Outdoor life goes on as usual throughout winter when horseback riding, outdoor swimming, and snow adventure activities take on an added element of excitement under the shimmering Northern Lights. Temps average in the low 30sF.

Spring arrives in April or May when temperatures begin to warm up. This is the best time to find travel deals. Fishing, whale watching and golf season begin, and migratory birds return. Temps average in the low 40sF.

Summer arrives in June. The meadows are a brilliant green, and Viking horses and sheep roam the countryside. Summers in Iceland can be pleasantly warm (never hot!) and the Midnight Sun bring extended daylight. This is peak season for tourists and activities, such as hiking, biking, and horseback riding. Temps average in the low 50sF.

Fall begins in September. Late fall is peak Northern Lights Season and many festivals are held during this time of year. Adventure activities are abundant, including cave tours and glacier tours. Temps average in the 40sF.

FYI: In Iceland gratuity is always included in the bill, so tipping is not required. This applies to everything: restaurants, taxis, cafés, room service and more. However, if you do feel that you have received great service, Icelanders appreciate a tip and will gladly accept it. Value Added Tax (VAT) in Iceland is 24% or 11% on certain items. A refund of the local VAT is available to visitors and will result in a reduction of up to 15% of the retail price provided departure from Iceland is within 30 days after the purchase is made. The purchased amount must be no less than 4,000 ISK (VAT included) per sales receipt. Refunds can be collected in the departures hall of Keflavik International Airport. For more information about VAT, http://www.iceland.is/iceland-abroad/be/tourist-information/vat-refund---tax-free/

What to Pack

The key to dressing for Iceland's climate is layering, regardless of the season. Wear clothing, such as a sweater, multi-purpose vest (like a safari vest), or jacket that can be discarded during the warmest part of the day. I like to wear convertible pants that can be "unzipped" to become shorts and easily converted back to long pants late in the day. Casual clothes are acceptable almost everywhere.

Lightweight woolens, rain- and windproof jacket & trousers, and good walking/hiking shoes are essential if you plan to do any nature tours.

If traveling in the winter, bring a warm all-weather overcoat, hat, scarf, gloves, socks (preferably made of wool) as well a sweater, and weatherproof shoes. Long thermal underwear (a shirt and pants), and a layer of fleece on top.

In summer, always carry a lightweight, water-resistant jacket.

Sturdy walking shoes for trekking & hiking are needed. Sometimes rubber boots may be necessary. For adventure activities, you will usually be provided with gear, such as a snow suit. At the very least, the company will provide you with a list of suggested gear, such as gloves or boots.

Be sure to bring a bathing suit and a cover-up. You will need them at the Blue Lagoon. Also, there are year-round geothermal pools, and you may want to visit a day spa or use your hotel or guest house hot tub.

Be sure to bring a waterproof camera or recorder if you want to take photos or video. At the very least, pack electronic equipment in a waterproof bag. Remember that you will be close up to geysers, waterfalls, lagoons, etc. You should keep your important documents, such as tickets, money, and passports, in a waterproof bag.

If you're going to be camping or renting a property, make sure to find out if you need to bring or rent towels, sleeping bags, linen, etc.

I carry large plastic zip top bags so I can store wet bathing suits or dirty shoes. Also, I can safely store snacks and my important documents in these clear, plastic bags so I can easily find what I need in a hurry.

If you wear glasses, bring a spare pair. If you take medication, bring enough to last three or four days longer than your trip, in case you get delayed.

TERRANCE ZEPKE
Series Reading Order & Guide

TERRANCE TALKS TRAVEL: The Quirky Tourist Guide to Reykjavik | Terrance Zepke

Series List

Most Haunted Series
Terrance Talks Travel Series
Cheap Travel Series
Spookiest Series
Stop Talking Series
Carolinas for Kids Series
Ghosts of the Carolinas Series
Books & Guides for the Carolinas Series
& More Books by Terrance Zepke

≈

Introduction

Here is a list of titles by Terrance Zepke. They are presented in chronological order although they do not need to be read in any particular order.

Also included is an author bio, a personal message from Terrance, and some other information you may find helpful.

All books are available as eBooks and print books. They can be found on all major booksellers or through your favorite independent bookseller.

For more about this author and her books visit her Author Page at: http://www.amazon.com/Terrance-Zepke/e/B000APJNIA/.

You can also connect with Terrance on Twitter @terrancezepke or on

www.facebook.com/terrancezepke
www.pinterest.com/terrancezepke
www.goodreads.com/terrancezepke

TERRANCE TALKS TRAVEL: The Quirky Tourist Guide to Reykjavik | Terrance Zepke

Sign up for weekly email notifications of the ***Terrance Talks Travel*** blog and receive a FREE 50-page CHEAP TRAVEL REPORT and be the first to learn about new episodes of Uber Adventures, cheap travel tips & resources, and her TRIP PICK OF THE WEEK at www.terrancetalkstravel.com or sign up for her ***Mostly Ghostly*** blog at www.terrancezepke.com.

≈

You can follow her travel show, **TERRANCE TALKS TRAVEL: ÜBER ADVENTURES** on <u>www.blogtalkradio.com/terrancetalkstravel</u> or subscribe to it on **iTunes.**

Warning: Listening to this show could lead to a spectacular South African safari, hot-air ballooning over the Swiss Alps, Disney Adventures, and Tornado Tours!

TERRANCE TALKS TRAVEL: The Quirky Tourist Guide to Reykjavik | Terrance Zepke

Terrance Zepke is co-host of the writing show, **A WRITER'S JOURNEY: FROM BLANK PAGE TO PUBLISHED.** All episodes can be found on **iTunes** or **www.terrancezepke.com.**

≈

AUTHOR BIO

Terrance Zepke studied Journalism at the University of Tennessee and later received a Master's degree in Mass Communications from the University of South Carolina. She studied parapsychology at the renowned Rhine Research Center.

Zepke spends much of her time happily traveling around the world but always returns home to the Carolinas where she lives part-time in both states. She has written hundreds of articles and close to three dozen books. She is the host of *Terrance Talks Travel: Über Adventures* and co-host of *A Writer's Journey: From Blank Page to Published*. Additionally, this award-winning and best-selling author has been featured in many publications and programs, such as NPR, CNN, The Washington Post, Associated Press, Travel with Rick Steves, Around the World, Publishers Weekly, World Travel & Dining with Pierre Wolfe, Good Morning Show, The Learning Channel, and The Travel Channel.

When she's not investigating haunted places, searching for pirate treasure, or climbing lighthouses, she is most likely packing for her next adventure to some far flung place, such as Entebbe or Kwazulu Natal. Some of her favorite adventures include piranha fishing on the Amazon, seeing the Aurora Borealis in Reykjavik, shark cage diving in South Africa, hiking the Andes Mountains Inca Trail, camping in the Himalayas, dog-sledding in the Arctic Circle, and a gorilla safari in the Congo.

≈

MOST HAUNTED SERIES

A Ghost Hunter's Guide to the Most Haunted Places in America (2012)
https://read.amazon.com/kp/embed?asin=B0085SG22O&preview=newtab&linkCode=kpe&ref_=cm_sw_r_kb_dp_zerQwb1AMJ0R4

A Ghost Hunter's Guide to the Most Haunted Houses in America (2013)
https://read.amazon.com/kp/embed?asin=B00C3PUMGC&preview=newtab&linkCode=kpe&ref_=cm_sw_r_kb_dp_BfrQwb1WF1Y6T

A Ghost Hunter's Guide to the Most Haunted Hotels & Inns in America (2014)
https://read.amazon.com/kp/embed?asin=B00C3PUMGC&preview=newtab&linkCode=kpe

A Ghost Hunter's Guide to the Most Haunted Historic Sites in America (2016)

https://read.amazon.com/kp/embed?asin=B01LXADK90&preview=newtab&linkCode=kpe&ref_=cm_sw_r_kb_dp_WFFLybJ2TWGAR

The Ghost Hunter's MOST HAUNTED Box Set (3 in 1): Discover America's Most Haunted Destinations (2016)

https://read.amazon.com/kp/embed?asin=B01HISAAJM&preview=newtab&linkCode=kpe&ref_=cm_sw_r_kb_dp_AGFLybMNFJKBA

TERRANCE TALKS TRAVEL: The Quirky Tourist Guide to Reykjavik l Terrance Zepke

MOST HAUNTED and SPOOKIEST Sampler Box Set: Featuring *A GHOST HUNTER'S GUIDE TO THE MOST HAUNTED PLACES IN AMERICA* and *SPOOKIEST CEMETERIES* (2017)

https://read.amazon.com/kp/embed?asin=B01N17EEOM&preview=newtab&linkCode=kpe&ref_=cm_sw_r_kb_dp_.JFLybCTN3QEF

A Ghost Hunter's Guide to the Most Haunted Places in the World (2018)
https://read.amazon.com/kp/embed?asin=B078ZL382D&preview=newtab&linkCode=kpe&ref_=cm_sw_r_kb_dp_nVNXAb61HF42W

≈

TERRANCE TALKS TRAVEL: The Quirky Tourist Guide to Reykjavik | Terrance Zepke

TERRANCE TALKS TRAVEL SERIES

Terrance Talks Travel: A Pocket Guide to South Africa (2015)
https://read.amazon.com/kp/embed?asin=B00PSTFTLI&preview=newtab&linkCode=kpe&ref_=cm_sw_r_kb_dp_pirQwb12XZX65

Terrance Talks Travel: A Pocket Guide to African Safaris (2015)
https://read.amazon.com/kp/embed?asin=B00PSTFZSA&preview=newtab&linkCode=kpe&ref_=cm_sw_r_kb_dp_jhrQwb0P8Z87G

Terrance Talks Travel: A Pocket Guide to Adventure Travel (2015)
https://read.amazon.com/kp/embed?asin=B00UKMAVQG&preview=newtab&linkCode=kpe&ref_=cm_sw_r_kb_dp_ThrQwb1PVVZAZ

Terrance Talks Travel: A Pocket Guide to Florida Keys (including Key West & The Everglades) (2016)
https://read.amazon.com/kp/embed?asin=B01EWHML58&preview=newtab&linkCode=kpe&ref_=cm_sw_r_kb_dp_YMbHybP0ZZEFK

Terrance Talks Travel: The Quirky Tourist Guide to Key West (2017)

TERRANCE TALKS TRAVEL: The Quirky Tourist Guide to Reykjavik I Terrance Zepke

https://read.amazon.com/kp/embed?asin=B01N3BF80O&preview=newtab&linkCode=kpe&ref_=cm_sw_r_kb_dp_wHFLyb1F89GNR

Terrance Talks Travel: The Quirky Tourist Guide to Cape Town (2017)

https://read.amazon.com/kp/embed?asin=B01N6YKI77&preview=newtab&linkCode=kpe&ref_=cm_sw_r_kb_dp_jIFLybNCTJ5NN

African Safari Box Set: Featuring TERRANCE TALKS TRAVEL: *A Pocket Guide to South Africa* and *TERRANCE TALKS TRAVEL: A Pocket Guide to African Safaris* (2017)
https://read.amazon.com/kp/embed?asin=B01MUH6VJU&preview=newtab&linkCode=kpe&ref_=cm_sw_r_kb_dp_xLFLybAQKFA0B

Terrance Talks Travel: The Quirky Tourist Guide to Reykjavik (2017)
https://www.amazon.com/Terrance-Zepke/e/B000APJNIA/ref=sr_ntt_srch_lnk_15?qid=1488514258&sr=8-15

Terrance Talks Travel: The Quirky Tourist Guide to Charleston, South Carolina (2017)
https://www.amazon.com/Terrance-Zepke/e/B000APJNIA/ref=sr_ntt_srch_lnk_15?qid=1488514258&sr=8-15

TERRANCE TALKS TRAVEL: The Quirky Tourist Guide to Reykjavik I Terrance Zepke

Terrance Talks Travel: The Quirky Tourist Guide to Ushuaia (2017)
https://www.amazon.com/Terrance-Zepke/e/B000APJNIA/ref=sr_ntt_srch_lnk_15?qid=1488514258&sr=8-15

Terrance Talks Travel: The Quirky Tourist Guide to Antarctica (2017) https://www.amazon.com/Terrance-Zepke/e/B000APJNIA/ref=sr_ntt_srch_lnk_1?qid=1489092624&sr=8-1

TERRANCE TALKS TRAVEL: The Quirky Tourist Guide to Machu Picchu & Cuzco (Peru) 2017
https://read.amazon.com/kp/embed?asin=B07147HLQY&preview=newtab&linkCode=kpe&ref_=cm_sw_r_kb_dp_HmZmzb9FT5E0P

Terrance Talks Travel: A Pocket Guide to East Africa's Uganda and Rwanda (2018)
https://read.amazon.com/kp/embed?asin=B079YN892B&preview=newtab&linkCode=kpe&ref_=cm_sw_r_kb_dp_RWvQAbR3KQVQM

TERRANCE TALKS TRAVEL: The Quirky Tourist Guide to Kathmandu (Nepal) & The Himalayas (2018)
https://www.amazon.com/Terrance-Zepke/e/B000APJNIA/ref=dp_byline_cont_ebooks_1

TERRANCE TALKS TRAVEL: The Quirky Tourist Guide to Reykjavik | Terrance Zepke

African Safari Box Set: Featuring TERRANCE TALKS TRAVEL: *A Pocket Guide to South Africa* and *TERRANCE TALKS TRAVEL: A Pocket Guide to African Safaris* (2017)
https://read.amazon.com/kp/embed?asin=B01MUH6VJU&preview=newtab&linkCode=kpe&ref_=cm_sw_r_kb_dp_xLFLybAQKFA0B

≈

TERRANCE TALKS TRAVEL: The Quirky Tourist Guide to Reykjavik | Terrance Zepke

CHEAP TRAVEL SERIES

How to Cruise Cheap! (2017)

https://read.amazon.com/kp/embed?asin=B01N6NYM1N&preview=newtab&linkCode=kpe&ref_=cm_sw_r_kb_dp_6DFLybR27HH38

How to Fly Cheap! (2017)

https://read.amazon.com/kp/embed?asin=B01N7Q81YG&preview=newtab&linkCode=kpe&ref_=cm_sw_r_kb_dp_5EFLybR6GNNHD

How to Travel Cheap! (2017)

https://www.amazon.com/Terrance-Zepke/e/B000APJNIA/

How to Travel FREE or Get Paid to Travel! (2017)

https://www.amazon.com/Terrance-Zepke/e/B000APJNIA/

CHEAP TRAVEL SERIES (4 IN 1) BOX SET (2017)
https://read.amazon.com/kp/embed?asin=B071ZGV1TY&preview=newtab&linkCode=kpe&ref_=cm_sw_r_kb_dp_.VNXAb8HMFQDY

≈

SPOOKIEST SERIES

Spookiest Lighthouses (2013)
https://read.amazon.com/kp/embed?asin=B00EAAQA2S
&preview

Spookiest Battlefields (2015)
https://read.amazon.com/kp/embed?asin=B00XUSWS3
G&preview=newtab&linkCode=kpe&ref_=cm_sw_r_kb
_dp_okrQwb0TR9F8M

Spookiest Cemeteries (2016)

https://read.amazon.com/kp/embed?asin=B01D0FP498&
preview=newtab&linkCode=kpe&ref_=cm_sw_r_kb_dp
_wJFLyb3X9XSK7

Spookiest Box Set (3 in 1): Discover America's Most Haunted Destinations (2016)
https://read.amazon.com/kp/embed?asin=B01HH2OM4I
&preview=newtab&linkCode=kpe&ref_=cm_sw_r_kb_
dp_Anz-xbT3SDEZS

MOST HAUNTED and SPOOKIEST Sampler Box Set: Featuring *A GHOST HUNTER'S GUIDE TO THE MOST HAUNTED PLACES IN AMERICA* and *SPOOKIEST CEMETERIES* (2017)

https://read.amazon.com/kp/embed?asin=B01N17EEOM
&preview=newtab&linkCode=kpe&ref_=cm_sw_r_kb_
dp_.JFLybCTN3QEF

TERRANCE TALKS TRAVEL: The Quirky Tourist Guide to Reykjavik | Terrance Zepke

Spookiest Objects (2017)
https://read.amazon.com/kp/embed?asin=B0728FMVZF&preview=newtab&linkCode=kpe&ref_=cm_sw_r_kb_dp_TXNXAbS0DF352

≈

STOP TALKING SERIES

Stop Talking & Start Writing Your Book (2015)
https://read.amazon.com/kp/embed?asin=B012YHTIAY
&preview=newtab&linkCode=kpe&ref_=cm_sw_r_kb_
dp_qlrQwb1N7G3YF

Stop Talking & Start Publishing Your Book (2015)
https://read.amazon.com/kp/embed?asin=B013HHV1LE
&preview=newtab&linkCode=kpe&ref_=cm_sw_r_kb_
dp_WlrQwb1F63MFD

Stop Talking & Start Selling Your Book (2015)
https://read.amazon.com/kp/embed?asin=B015YAO33K
&preview=newtab&linkCode=kpe&ref_=cm_sw_r_kb_
dp_ZkrQwb188J8BE

Stop Talking & Start Writing Your Book Series (3 in 1) Box Set (2016)

https://read.amazon.com/kp/embed?asin=B01M58J5AZ
&preview=newtab&linkCode=kpe&ref_=cm_sw_r_kb_
dp_4MFLybYA8CP9F

≈

TERRANCE TALKS TRAVEL: The Quirky Tourist Guide to
Reykjavik | Terrance Zepke

CAROLINAS FOR KIDS SERIES

Lighthouses of the Carolinas for Kids (2009)
http://www.amazon.com/Lighthouses-Carolinas-Kids-Terrance-Zepke/dp/1561644293/ref=asap_bc?ie=UTF8

Pirates of the Carolinas for Kids (2009)
https://read.amazon.com/kp/embed?asin=B01BJ3VSWK&preview=newtab&linkCode=kpe&ref_=cm_sw_r_kb_dp_rGrXwb0XDTSTA

Ghosts of the Carolinas for Kids (2011)
https://read.amazon.com/kp/embed?asin=B01BJ3VSVQ&preview=newtab&linkCode=kpe&ref_=cm_sw_r_kb_dp_XLrXwb0E7N1AK

≈

TERRANCE TALKS TRAVEL: The Quirky Tourist Guide to Reykjavik I Terrance Zepke

GHOSTS OF THE CAROLINAS SERIES

Ghosts of the Carolina Coasts (1999)
http://www.amazon.com/Ghosts-Carolina-Coasts-Terrance-Zepke/dp/1561641758/ref=asap_bc?ie=UTF8

The Best Ghost Tales of South Carolina (2004)
http://www.amazon.com/Best-Ghost-Tales-South-Carolina/dp/1561643068/ref=asap_bc?ie=UTF8

Ghosts & Legends of the Carolina Coasts (2005)
https://read.amazon.com/kp/embed?asin=B01AGQJABW&preview=newtab&linkCode=kpe&ref_=cm_sw_r_kb_dp_VKrXwb1Q09794

The Best Ghost Tales of North Carolina (2006)
https://read.amazon.com/kp/embed?asin=B01BJ3VSV6&preview=newtab&linkCode=kpe&ref_=cm_sw_r_kb_dp_6IrXwb0XKT90Q

≈

TERRANCE TALKS TRAVEL: The Quirky Tourist Guide to Reykjavik | Terrance Zepke

BOOKS & GUIDES FOR THE CAROLINAS SERIES

Pirates of the Carolinas (2005)
http://www.amazon.com/Pirates-Carolinas-Terrance-Zepke/dp/1561643440/ref=asap_bc?ie=UTF8

Coastal South Carolina: Welcome to the Lowcountry (2006)
http://www.amazon.com/Coastal-South-Carolina-Welcome-Lowcountry/dp/1561643483/ref=asap_bc?ie=UTF8

Coastal North Carolina: Its Enchanting Islands, Towns & Communities (2011)
http://www.amazon.com/Coastal-North-Carolina-Terrance-Zepke/dp/1561645117/ref=asap_bc?ie=UTF8

Lighthouses of the Carolinas: A Short History & Guide (2011)
https://read.amazon.com/kp/embed?asin=B01AGQJA7G&preview=newtab&linkCode=kpe&ref_=cm_sw_r_kb_dp_UHrXwb09A22P1

≈

TERRANCE TALKS TRAVEL: The Quirky Tourist Guide to Reykjavik I Terrance Zepke

MORE BOOKS BY TERRANCE ZEPKE

Lowcountry Voodoo: Tales, Spells & Boo Hags (2009)
https://read.amazon.com/kp/embed?asin=B018WAGUC6&preview=newtab&linkCode=kpe&ref_=cm_sw_r_kb_dp_UmrQwb19AVSYG

Ghosts of Savannah (2012)
http://www.amazon.com/Ghosts-Savannah-Terrance-Zepke/dp/1561645303/ref=asap_bc?ie=UTF8

How To Train Your Puppy or Dog Using Three Simple Strategies (FUN & FAST!) (2017)
https://read.amazon.com/kp/embed?asin=B01MZ5GN2M&preview=newtab&linkCode=kpe&ref_=cm_sw_r_kb_dp_bQFLyb76G2KYW

*Fiction books were written under a pseudonym.

≈

TERRANCE TALKS TRAVEL: The Quirky Tourist Guide to Reykjavik | Terrance Zepke

Message from the Author

The primary purpose of this guide is to introduce you to some titles you may not have known about. Another reason for it is to let you know all the ways you can connect with me. Authors love to hear from readers. We truly appreciate you more than you'll ever know. Please feel free to send me a comment or question via the comment form found on every page on www.terrancezepke.com and www.terrancetalkstravel.com or follow me on your favorite social media. Don't forget that you can also listen to my writing podcast on iTunes, **A Writer's Journey**, or my travel show, **Terrance Talks Travel: Über Adventures** on Blog Talk Radio and iTunes. The best way to make sure you don't miss any episodes of these shows (and find a complete archive of shows), new book releases and giveaways, contests, my TRIP PICK OF THE WEEK, cheap travel tips, free downloadable travel reports, and more is to subscribe to *Terrance Talks Travel* on www.terrancetalkstravel.com or *Mostly Ghostly* on www.terrancezepke.com. If you'd like to learn more about any of my books, you can find in-depth descriptions and "look inside" options through most online booksellers. Also, please note that links to book previews have been included in SERIES section of this booklet for your convenience.

Thank you for your interest and HAPPY READING!

Terrance

INDEX

A

Adventure, 3, 27, 56, 123, 139
Akureyri Golf Club, 63
annual events, 101
Arctic Circle, 122
Arctic Open, 63
Aurora Borealis, 26
Aurora Reykjavik, 28

B

Blue Lagoon, 3, 7, 20, 25, 67, 82, 127

C

Christmas, 16, 35, 111, 112, 114, 115, 116, 117, 118
Christmas Cave, 116
Christmas Market, 114
Citywalk, 58

D

Denmark, 96

E

Elf School, 31
Ellidaardalur Valley, 39
Europe, 3, 9, 29, 41, 62, 66, 94, 101
Eyjafjallajökull, 100

F

ferry, 11
Festival, 102, 103, 105, 106, 110

G

Glacier Lagoon, 22
Golden Circle, 18
Greenland, 94

H

Hafnarfjordur, 93
hákarl, 36
Hallgrímskirkja Church, 39
Harpa, 24
Harpa Concert & Conference Center, 41
Heidmark Christmas Market, 114
Höfði House, 42
Hverageroi, 19

I

Ice Cave Tour, 59
Iceland, 1, 3, 4, 6, 7, 9, 11, 12, 14, 15, 16, 17, 19, 20, 21, 23, 24, 25, 31, 32, 41, 43, 46, 50, 52, 54, 58, 59, 61, 62, 63, 65, 66, 67, 76, 82, 83, 86, 89, 90, 91, 92, 94, 97, 101, 103, 104, 105, 106, 109, 110, 111, 113, 117, 119, 120, 121, 123, 124, 125
Icelandair, 10
Icelandic folklore, 31, 38, 93
Icelandic horses, 119
Icelandic Króna, 14

Imagine Peace Tower, 55

J

Jólakrás Street Food Christmas Market, 114

K

Keflavik International Airport, 9
Kerio Volcanic Crater Lake, 19

L

Langjokull, 59
Laugardalur Valley
   Hot Spring Valley, 44
Leifur Eriksson, 97

M

Museum of Icelandic Sorcery & Witchcraft, 30

N

Nautholsvik Geothermal Beach, 47
New Year's Eve, 113
North Atlantic Ocean, 119
Northern Lights. *See* Aurora Borealis

P

Phallological Museum, 53
Puffin Tour, 60

R

Republic of Iceland. *See* Iceland

Reykjavik, 1, 3, 4, 8, 9, 12, 17, 18, 20, 27, 28, 39, 44, 48, 51, 52, 53, 54, 58, 59, 60, 62, 63, 64, 70, 74, 76, 77, 81, 82, 83, 84, 87, 88, 90, 91, 92, 95, 100, 102, 103, 105, 106, 107, 108, 109, 110, 111, 114, 119, 122, 136, 140
Reykjavík Art Museum, 53
Reykjavík City Hall, 115
Reykjavik City Museum, 53
Reykjavik Flea Market, 81
Reykjavik Food Walk, 60
Reykjavik International Airport, 9
Ring Road, 19
RÚNTUR, 74

S

Seljalandsfoss Waterfall, 68
Snaefellsness Peninsula, 48
Strokkur Geyser, 66
Summer Solstice, 107

T

The National Museum of Iceland, 50
The Pearl, 51
Thingvellir, 23

Þ

Þingvellir, 23

T

Thorrablot, 102

U

Union Treaty, 98

V

Value Added Tax, 124
VAT. *See* Value Added Tax
Vatnajokull, 59
Vatnajokull Glacier, 66
Videy Island, 54
visa
 tourist, 15
Vopnafjördur, 22

W

Westman Islands, 46

Y

Your Friend in Reykjavik, 62
Yule Town, 114

Made in the USA
Columbia, SC
24 July 2019